NATURAL DISASTERS

Flood Damage

Susan Bullen

Wayland

Natural Disasters

A Storm Rages
A Volcano Erupts
Flood Damage
The Power of
Earthquakes

165092

Editor: Deb Elliott
Designer: Malcolm Walker

Cover pictures: background – Crashing waves with white surf. left – Kutubra Island in the midst of the flood which claimed nineteen lives. middle – A storm in Guadeloupe caused flooding and severe damage. right – A house submerged in water after floods in the American state of Arkansas.

Text is based on *Flood* in *The Violent Earth* series published in 1992
First published in 1994 by
Wayland (Publishers) Ltd
61 Western Road, Hove
East Sussex, BN3 1JD, England

British Library Cataloguing in Publication Data
Bullen, Susan
  Flood Damage. - (Natural Disasters Series)
  I. Title II. Series
  551.48

ISBN 0 7502 1188 1

Typeset by Kudos
Printed and bound by
  Rotolito Lombarda s.p.a.

Contents

◄ *This is a flooded village in Sudan, Africa.*

Floods hit China

Look at this street in Wuxi in China. People are wading through deep water. That's because Wuxi was hit by a huge flood in July 1991. There was water everywhere!

▼ *This flooded street in Wuxi looks more like a river.*

Here are some of the worst floods to hit China since 1900		
Year	Name of river	People killed
1931	Yellow River	3.7 million
1938	Yellow River	890,000
1954	Yangtze	30,000
1991	Yangtze	1,700

The Great Wall

Beijing •

MONGOLIA

CHINA

JAPAN

INDIA

0 ————— 500km

North China Plain

Lanzhou
•

Loess Plateau

Yellow River (Huang He)

Xian •

Yellow Sea

CHINA

Nanjing •
Shanghai •

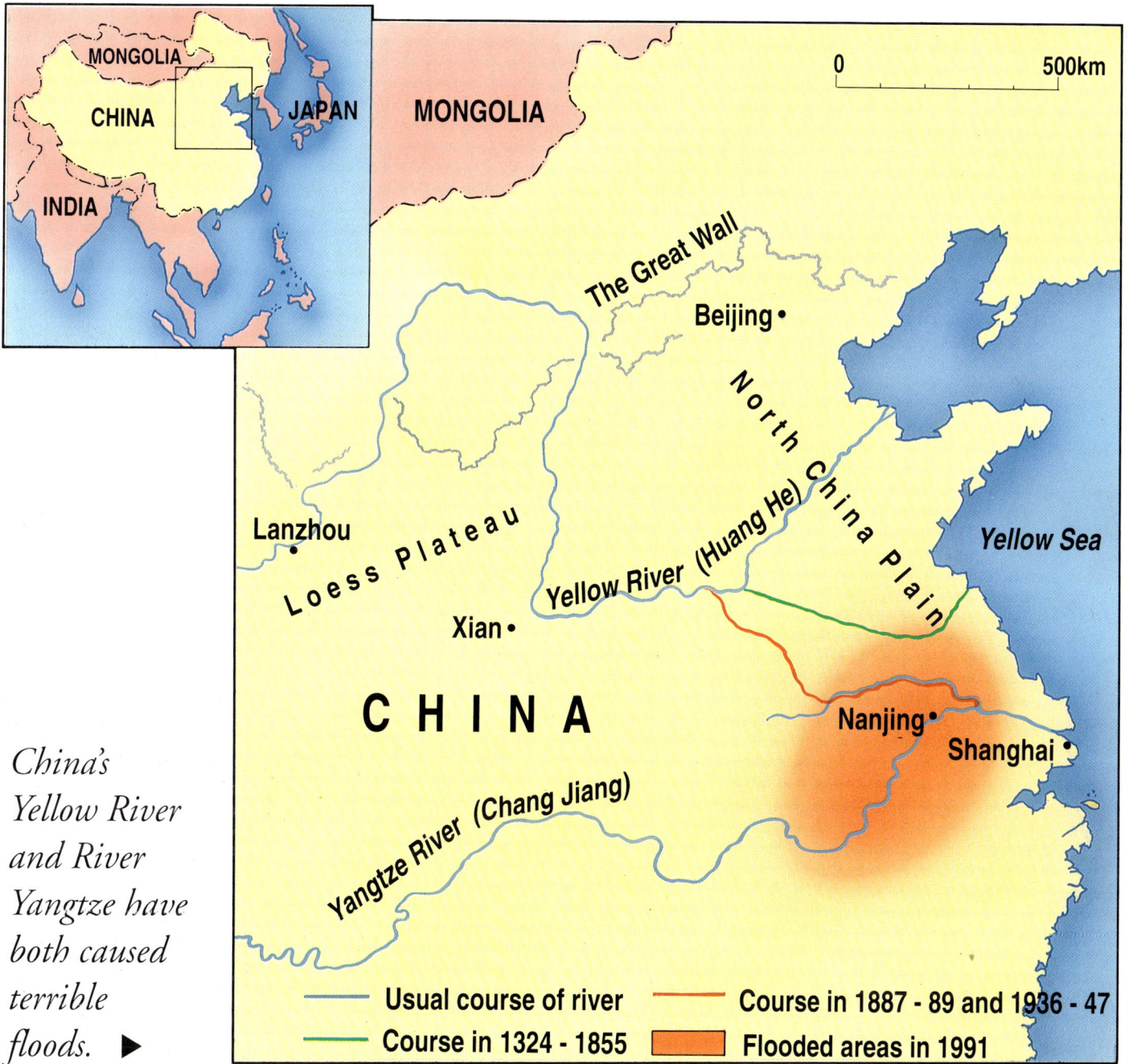

*China's
Yellow River
and River
Yangtze have
both caused
terrible
floods.* ▶

Yangtze River (Chang Jiang)

—— Usual course of river   —— Course in 1887 - 89 and 1936 - 47
—— Course in 1324 - 1855   ▮ Flooded areas in 1991

Wuxi is a city near the River Yangtze. In July 1991 there
was so much rain, the Yangtze burst its banks. The water
ruined many homes and swept some people away.

Floods from the River Yangtze ruined a huge area of rice fields. The floods mixed with people's drinking water, which made it unsafe to drink. When people drank the water, they became ill.

▼ *Can you see the concrete channels? They were built to take away extra water when the Yangtze floods.*

The Yangtze River has flooded many times. But China's most serious floods have been caused by the Yellow River. Now people are trying to make both rivers safer.

Rivers can change

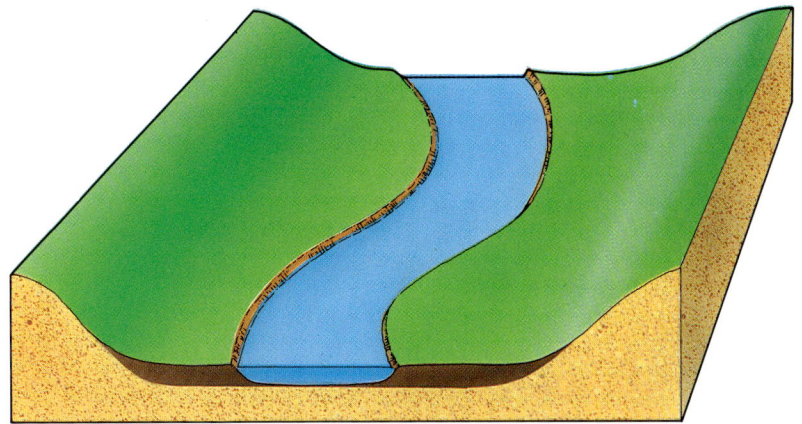

1 As a river flows along, it drops sandy soil along its edges.

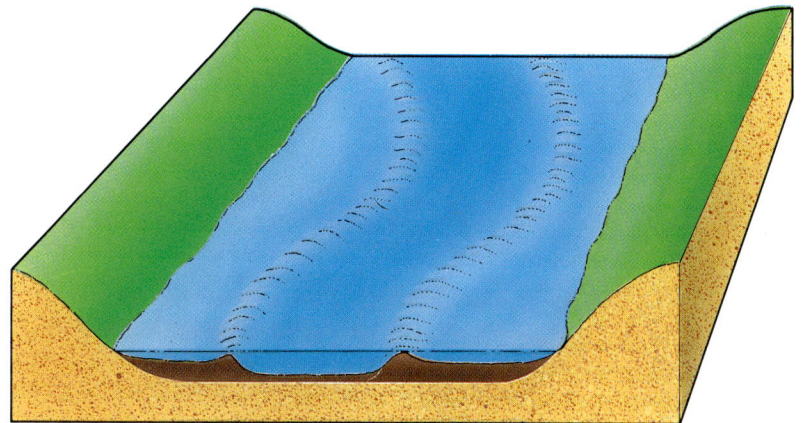

2 After many floods, ridges of sandy soil build up. We call them levees.

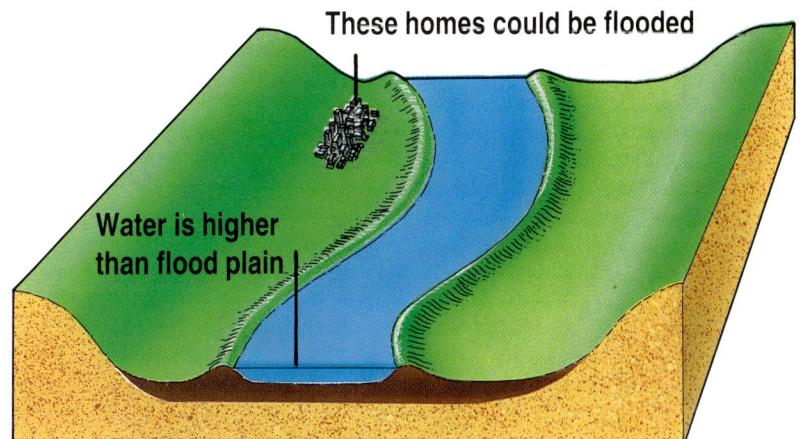

These homes could be flooded

Water is higher than flood plain

3 The sandy soil keeps piling up. Then the river is higher than the land next to it.

How do floods start?

Most floods happen quickly and suddenly. A river swells and the water spills on to dry land.

▼ *All these conditions can make floods happen.*

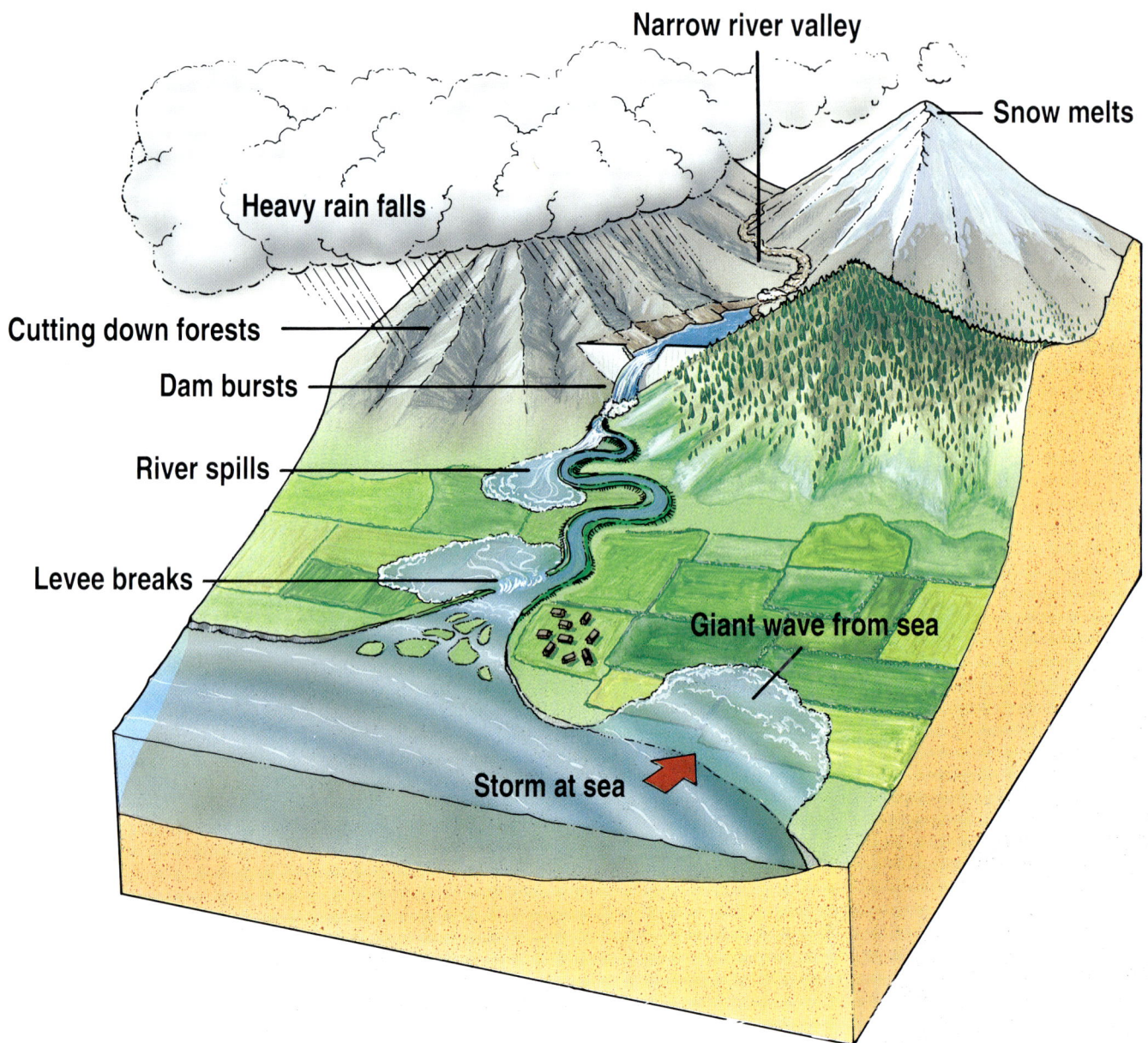

Narrow river valley

Snow melts

Heavy rain falls

Cutting down forests

Dam bursts

River spills

Levee breaks

Giant wave from sea

Storm at sea

▲ *Look at this huge wave. It causes flooding on land.*

Floods often come after heavy rain. In spring, floods happen when snow melts as the weather gets warmer. The melted snow makes a lot of extra water. Some floods are made by the sea. In stormy weather, huge waves can rush in and flood land at the coast.

Floods are dangerous

A tiny raindrop will not harm you. But a lot of water is very dangerous. Have you seen a big, fast-flowing river? So much water is very heavy and powerful.

▼ *These cars were swept along and smashed by a flood in France.*

▲ *Look at all this floodwater. It has knocked down a telephone box and flooded this house.*

Flood disasters

There are lots of big rivers in the USA. They have flooded many times in the past. The Mississippi and Missouri Rivers are both over 3,500 km long. After heavy rains, they can cause terrible floods.

▼ *An original photograph of the Mississippi flood in 1927.*

Minneapolis

Rocky Mountains

Missouri

Denver

Chicago

Ohio

Arkansas

Memphis

Mississippi

Appalachian Mountains

New York

Washington

Atlantic Ocean

New Orleans

Gulf of Mexico

0   500 km

Mississippi drainage basin

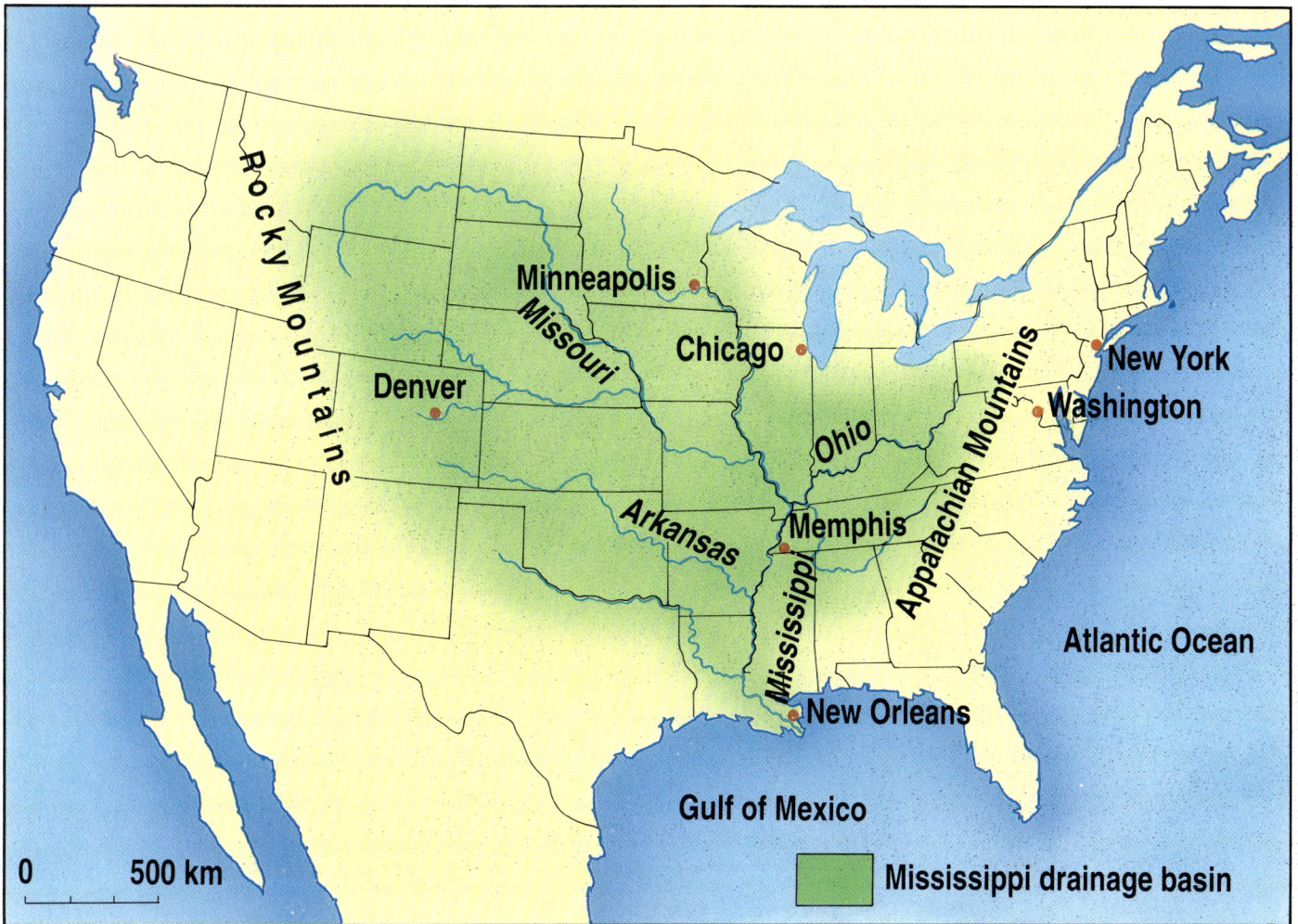

Floods in the Mississippi River Basin

1927 Mississippi floods:
      300 people killed
1951 Kansas and
      Missouri flood:
      41 people killed
1993 Mississippi and
      Missouri flood:
      41 people killed

▲   *This map shows the biggest rivers in the USA. They all flow into the Mississippi and then into the sea. When these rivers overflow, they flood a very big area.*

In July 1993 heavy rains made the Mississippi and Missouri Rivers flood again. The floods brought chaos to the state of Iowa and killed forty-one people.

In 1970 a storm called a cyclone hit Bangladesh, a small country near India. Giant waves higher than a house swept in from the sea. The great tide killed 40,000 people and ruined crops. Many more people died from diseases.

This family lost everything in the 1970 cyclone. ▶

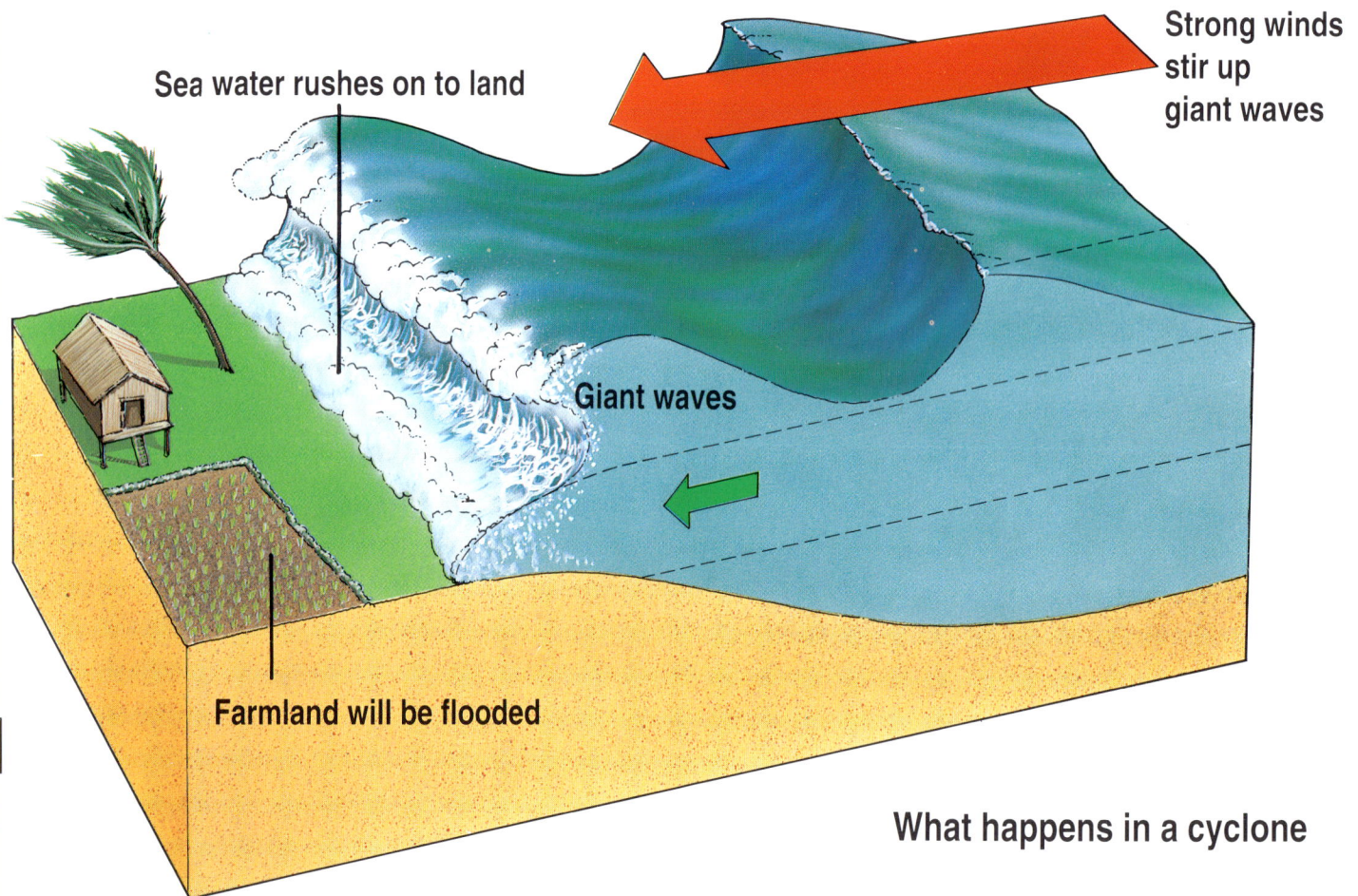

Sea water rushes on to land

Strong winds stir up giant waves

Giant waves

Farmland will be flooded

What happens in a cyclone

▲ *After a flood, it is hard to stay above the water level.*

In Bangladesh millions of people live by the big rivers called the Ganges and Brahmaputra. Whenever a cyclone comes, these people are in great danger from flooding. Floods happen almost every year.

In July 1976, the Big Thompson River in the USA overflowed. It was 7 metres high after a rainstorm. The swollen river rushed through a mountain gorge and swept away buildings, roads and cars and caused the deaths of 145 people.

▼ *This house was swept away by the Big Thompson River in 1976.*

'I'm trying to get out of here before I drown' said one man as the flood waters rose.

▲ *People in this Australian town try to carry on with their lives after flooding.*

Bad floods also happened in Australia in 1974. There were rainstorms even in the dry desert. The floods damaged 10,000 homes and killed many thousands of cows and sheep.

Floods in Europe			
Date	Place	Cause	People killed
1953	England and the Netherlands	Storm waves	2,157
1963	Alps, Italy	Burst dam	2,000
1966	Florence, Italy	River flood	127

In January 1953, storms blew over the North Sea in Europe. Huge waves hit the Netherlands and England. A huge tide nearly flooded London. In the Netherlands floods spread all over the low-lying land. They killed many people and farm animals.

Storm pushes the sea to the south

North Sea

ENGLAND

London

Dyke breaks

NETHERLANDS

BELGIUM

0   200 km

A man brings milk to an English home by boat in the 1953 flood. ▶

Helping after floods

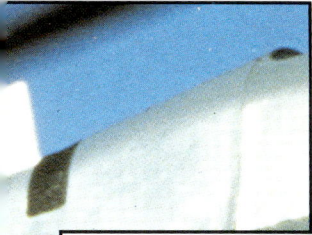

◄ *A helicopter rescues people from floods in France.*

After a flood, many people need help very quickly. They are homeless and have no food. They cannot even drink the water around them because it is dirty. So rescue workers bring them food, drink, clothes and shelter. Sometimes rescue workers come from many different countries to help after a flood.

◄ *Rescue workers brought food to people in Bangladesh after floods in 1988.*

Stopping floods

People who live near rivers are in danger from floods. But they have found some ways of making life safer.

▼   *These homes by the River Amazon in South America are built on stilts. This keeps the houses above the water level.*

Look at these bare slopes. Many trees have been cut down. ▶

▼ This man is planting young trees.

Trees can help stop floods. They break up the soil and water soon goes down to their roots. We can help by planting more trees. But cutting down trees helps floods to happen.

▼ *This is the Thames Barrier. It has strong gates which protect London from floods.*

Ways of stopping floods

Making high banks to keep out the water.
Building homes on high ground.
Changing the course of rivers.
Planting trees on steep, bare slopes.

▲ *A dam holds back water in a reservoir. This dam is in the Austrian mountains.*

Building a strong dam can control the flow of a river. When there is heavy rain, the extra water is stored behind the dam. The water stays in a lake called a reservoir. Later it is let out when people need the water.

Can floods help us?

Floods are not always bad. When a river overflows, it carries rich soil on to the land. The soil is good for growing crops.

▼ *These Chinese rice fields get water from channels which flow from the river.*

In Egypt, people have farmed land near the River Nile for thousands of years. The soil there is rich and good for growing crops. Now people have built a large dam on the Nile. There are no more floods and some farmers are sorry about this.

▼ *The Aswan High Dam in Egypt keeps the River Nile flowing steadily.*

Make a house on stilts

You can make a house on stilts, like the ones on page 22.

What to do:

1 Cut out a rectangle of cardboard for the base of the house. Carefully push a stick halfway through the base near each corner.

2 Cut out four cardboard rectangles for the walls. One pair should be longer than the other pair. Cut holes for the windows and door. Glue the walls to the base and to the sticks

3 Cut out two card rectangles and stick them on the roof.

4 Use Plasticine to stick a pebble on to each stick. Now stand your model house in a bowl of water. Make sure the floor level is above the water.

You need:
sticky tape or glue
cardboard
4 wooden sticks,
  20 centimetres long
4 pebbles
Plasticine
scissors

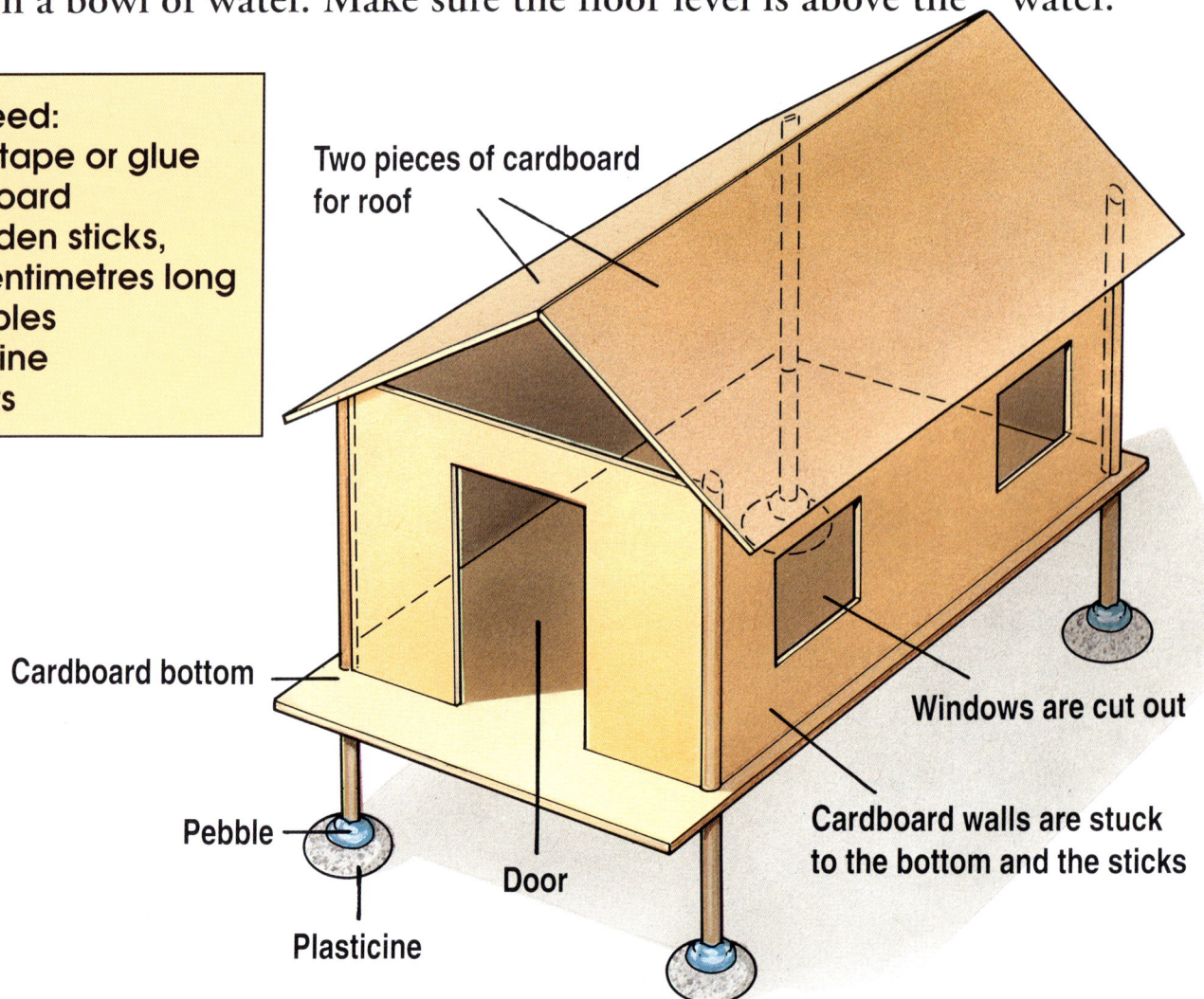

Two pieces of cardboard for roof

Cardboard bottom

Windows are cut out

Pebble

Cardboard walls are stuck to the bottom and the sticks

Door

Plasticine

Make a rain gauge

You can make a gauge and put it outside to measure rainfall.

What to do:

1 Cut a strip of paper and mark it with notches for centimetres. Tape this scale on to the jam jar. Fill this jar with 1 centimetre of water.

2 Stick a long strip of paper on to the thin jar. Pour the water from the jam jar into the thin jar. Mark the water level on the paper.
Label it 1 centimetre.

3 Do the same thing with 2 centimetres and 3 centimetres of water and repeat until the scale reaches the top of the thin jar. Empty the thin jar and write millimetres on to the scale.

4 Put the jam jar outside. Check it each day and pour any rainfall into the thin jar. Write down how many millimetres of rain have fallen.

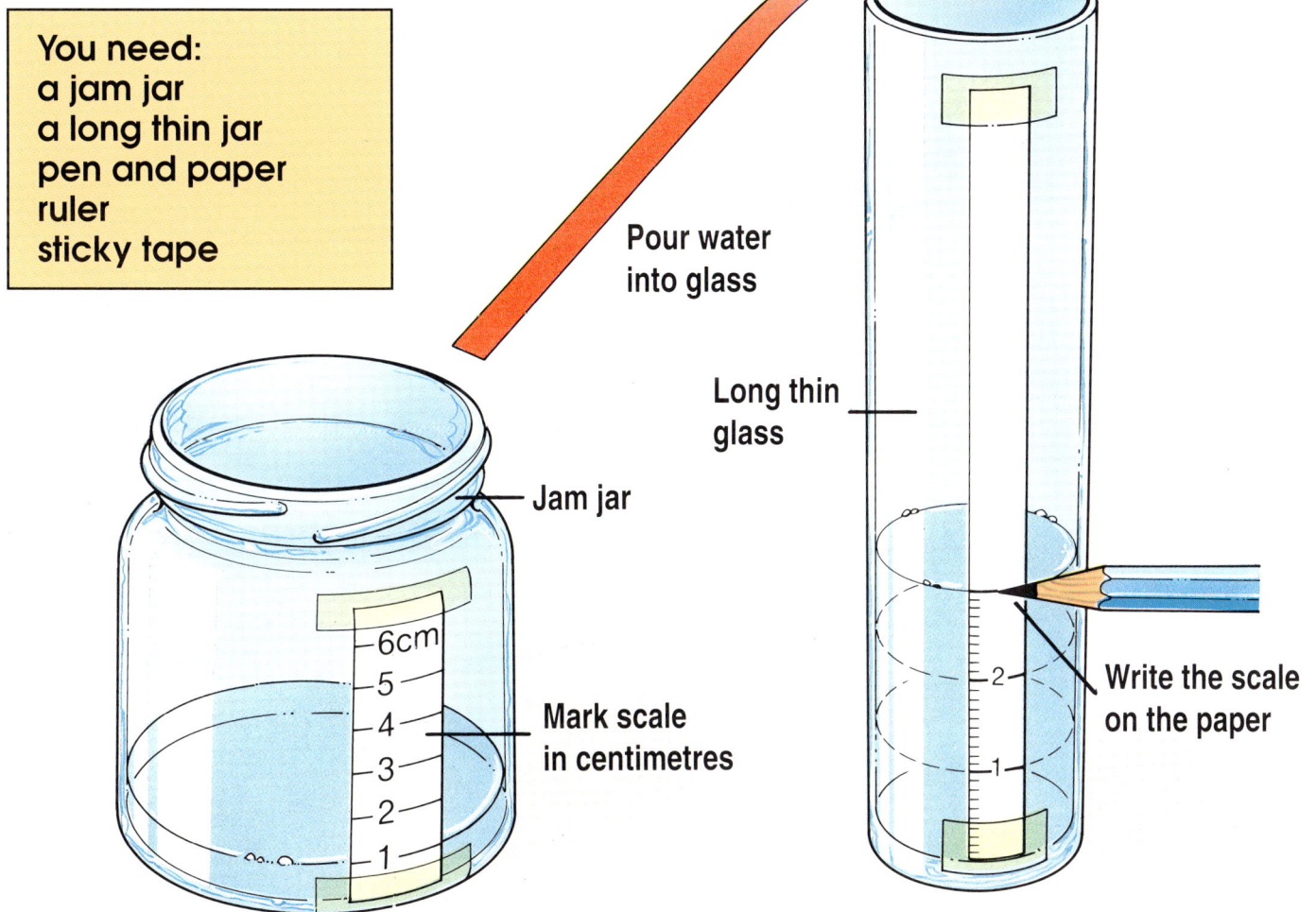

You need:
a jam jar
a long thin jar
pen and paper
ruler
sticky tape

Pour water into glass

Long thin glass

Jam jar

Mark scale in centimetres

6cm
5
4
3
2
1

Write the scale on the paper

2

1

Glossary

caused   Made happen.

channel   A ditch for water.

course   The route of a river.

cyclone   A strong, windy storm in hot parts of the world.

dam   A big wall that holds back stored water.

gorge   A narrow gap between steep rocks.

overflow   Spill over.

rescue workers   People who help others who are in danger.

survivor   A person who lives after a disaster.

tide   A strong flow from the sea.

wading   Walking through deep water.

Books to read

Flood by Brian Knapp
  (Macmillan, 1989)
Natural Disasters by Tim Wood
  (Wayland, 1993)
The Weather in Winter by Miriam Moss
  (Wayland, 1994)
Water by John Baines
  (Wayland, 1991)

Picture acknowledgements
The publisher would like to thank the following
for allowing their photographs to be reproduced in
this book: Camera Press 14 (top); Forestry
Commission 23 (bottom); Hutchison Library 6/7
Lyn Gambles; Panos Pictures 17 (Penny Tweedie),
21, 23 (top); Photri 9; Rex Features 2/3 (Roger
Hutchings), 4, 10, 10/11, 16, 20; Frank Spooner
cover (left, GAMMA/BARTHOLOMEW)(middle,
GAMMA/ Gary Williams)(right, GAMMA/ Dai
Jones); Tony Stone Worldwide cover (background,
Paul Berger); Topham Picture Library 12, 15, 19,
27; Julia Waterlow 22, 24, 26/7 (both); ZEFA
Picture Library 25.

Index